INDIANA

INDIANA

PHOTOGRAPHY BY DARRYL JONES

TEXT BY JARED CARTER

GRAPHIC ARTS CENTER PUBLISHING COMPANY PORTLAND, OREGON

To my wife, Nancy; my children, Aaron and Hannah;
my parents, Mr. and Mrs. William B. Jones, Jr.;
and my parents-in-law, Mr. and Mrs. C. William Grepp.

Darryl Jones

International Standard Book Number 0-912856-85-8
Library of Congress Catalog Card Number 83-83066
© MCMLXXXIV by Graphic Arts Center Publishing Company
P.O. Box 10306 • Portland, Oregon 97210 • 503/226-2402
Editor-in-Chief • Douglas A. Pfeiffer
Designer • Robert Reynolds
Typographer • Paul O. Giesey/Adcrafters
Printer • Bridgetown Printing
Bindery • Lincoln & Allen
Printed in the United States of America
Fourth Printing

Page 2: Speed, technology, courage, skill — they come together once each year during the 500-Mile Race at the Indianapolis Motor Speedway. Photographs of drivers, winning cars, and other memorabilia of "The Greatest Spectacle in Racing" may be visited year-round at the Hall of Fame Museum inside the track. The sleek red car was driven to victory in 1977 by A. J. Foyt, a four-time winner. In the 1948 Race, Duke Nalon drove the eight-cylinder supercharged Novi (foreground).

Right: The Soldiers and Sailors Monument, at the heart of Indianapolis on the Circle, commemorates Indiana's veterans in wars from 1776 to 1898.

Above: Summer fog mantling this Hoosier homestead north of Columbus may indicate that another scorcher is on the way. *Left:* A folk craftsman scrimshaws a powderhorn at one of the many encampments which annually celebrate Indiana's pioneer heritage. *Overleaf:* Lookout point, near the west entrance to Brown County State Park. Trees along the horizon mark the beginning of the 182,000-acre Hoosier National Forest, which extends from here to the Ohio River.

A wealth of steel mills, oil refineries, chemical plants, and extensive rail and harbor facilities make the Calumet Region in northwest Indiana a world leader in the production of industrial materials. Seen at sunset from Indiana Dunes State Park, the buildings and towers of Gary's industrial skyline thrust up above the waters of Lake Michigan.

Above: Long before Indiana's specialists in hybrid seed began experimenting with strains which would make the state one of the nation's leading producers of corn, native peoples cultivated many of their own varieties. These speckled ears hang in a roadside stand in the Brown County village of Beanblossom. *Overleaf:* A cloud-dappled day in rural DeKalb County, in the northeast part of the state.

Above: Near Michigan City, in Dunes State Park, wind and wave action have stripped Mount Baldy of all vegetation, moving it slowly southward, and burying an oak woodland in its path. *Right:* April in Brown County; blossoming redbud and dogwood in dense fog. *Overleaf:* Late spring or early summer, strangely pendulous mammatus clouds warn Hoosiers that tornadoes may be lurking nearby.

THE HOOSIER STATE

"It is decidedly un-Michigan-like," one Indiana writer suggested back in 1922 while ruminating about his home territory. "Although it tinges off toward Illinois on the west and Kentucky on the south, the community is neither nebulous nor indefinite. It is individual."

But what about Ohio, to the east—is it like Ohio? Ah yes, "the Buckeye State," said Indiana poet James Whitcomb Riley, "where a Hoosier is scrutinized as critically as a splinter in the thumb of a near-sighted man."

No, it is not at all like Ohio. Another Hoosier savant, Kin Hubbard, explained what happens when you cross the line from Ohio into Indiana: "I'm told by transcontinental tourists who cross Indianny west on the ole historic National road that they no sooner hit Richmond on the eastern border till plots fer novels an' rhymes fer verses come o'er 'em so fast an' thick that they kin hardly see the road, an' often go in the ditch."

Part of the Indiana legend is that practically everybody in the state is a writer. They tell outlandish stories about this. They claim that a visiting eastern writer once thought to coddle his Hoosier audience by inviting any local authors present to join him on the platform during his lecture—whereupon everyone in the audience stood up and moved forward.

They add that when he recovered from his shock and noticed one old man still seated at the back of the hall and inquired about him, the others said, "Oh, he writes too. He's just deaf and didn't hear what you said."

The truth is that the old man wasn't deaf, he was contrary. This is the chief Hoosier character trait, when all is said and done. Administer any sort of academic or journalistic poll, and Hoosiers will check off the boxes indicating that they are "shrewd," "independent," "conservative," "tradition-oriented," and so on. They do so because there is no box labeled "contrary."

I once knew an old farmer who lived up by Fortville who was contrary, in the classic sense. His name was Frosty Moore. "Frosty Moore is the salt of the earth," one of his neighbors announced one day while we were standing on an old trestle bridge, looking down at the water, "but he's so contrary, if he fell in the crick, he'd float upstream."

Hoosier contrariness is different from other forms. It is a mixture of stubbornness, skepticism, and occasional downright foolhardiness carried to such an outrageous degree that it reverses itself all over again and becomes sensible and calm.

Who else, in February of 1779, would have marched across Illinois country through two hundred miles of freezing, waist-high floodwaters to make a surprise attack on the British garrison at Vincennes? George Rogers Clark and his men did, and it worked, too. They weren't quite Hoosiers, since the state didn't exist yet. But the first chance they had, they settled in the territory. They were among the first to become Hoosiers by convincement.

Similarly, in the 1820s, who else would have built a governor's mansion inside a circle at the center of the newly surveyed capitol called Indianapolis and then elected a series of governors who absolutely refused to live in it? And who else, one hundred and fifty years later, would have built an enormous, domed sports stadium in downtown Indianapolis before having a major-league team to play in it? But Hoosiers liked the idea. When a contest was held to name the stadium, they sent in thousands of entry blanks insisting that it be called "The Hoosier Dome."

For that matter, who else would have laid out a two-and-a-half mile automobile racetrack where thirty-three cars go around in circles for five hundred miles but only once a year? Such things happen all the time in Indiana. Hoosier contrariness has its own logic.

Take the state's literature, of which the Hoosiers profess to be so proud. Probably the two most critically respected writers ever to come out of Indiana are Theodore Dreiser and Kurt Vonnegut, Jr. Throughout his career, Dreiser championed the poor and the disadvantaged. Vonnegut insists that his notions about world peace and disarmament were all acquired within a ten-mile radius of the Circle in Indianapolis where he grew up. Hoosiers respect their achievements but dislike their politics. Some are not willing to consider either writer as being quite representative of the state.

Possibly the two least critically respected writers ever to come out of Indiana are James Whitcomb Riley and Gene Stratton Porter. (She, in case you have forgotten, was the author of *Freckles*, *Laddie*, and *Girl of the Limberlost*.) Hoosiers cherish them dearly, maintaining not one but two restored homes, or shrines, for each writer. Riley's are in Greenfield and Indianapolis, in the central part of the state; Porter's are farther north, in Geneva and Rome City. This is contrariness of an advanced order. No other state could match it.

But then, no other state has a greater mystique, with the possible exception of Texas. Alongside the figure of the rangy, sunburned cowboy, dusty and ornery, and prone to the telling of tall tales, one may set the equally mythic figure of the backwoods Hoosier, gangly and rednecked, contrary rather than mean, neighborly when you finally get to know him, and also a teller of tall tales.

Abraham Lincoln, who was born in Kentucky but grew to manhood in southern Indiana, was just such a figure. Eugene Debs, the great Socialist leader from Terre Haute, was another. For contemporary examples, try Larry Bird of the Boston Celtics, choreographer Twyla Tharp, novelist Marilyn Durham, or Dave Letterman of late-night television.

Get any of them on a basketball court, too, and they'll shoot your socks off.

* * *

One of the more curious statistics about Indiana is that it produced more Mercury astronauts than any other state. Gus Grissom and Frank Borman, both among the nation's earliest space

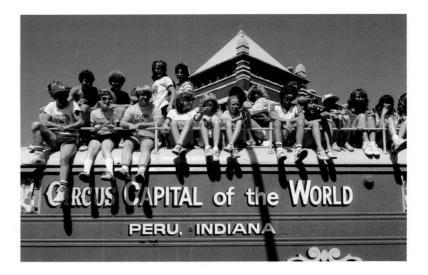

pioneers, were Hoosiers. Grissom and Tom Chaffee were Purdue graduates, as is Neil Armstrong, the first man to walk on the moon.

Yet if any of the Hoosiers who follow those explorers into space should pause in their labors above the earth and look down for a moment, hoping to locate the familiar thick-booted outline of Indiana, they would be disappointed. From a hundred miles up, the boundary lines would simply not be visible. Nor would anything else made by humans in Indiana. Instead, assuming no clouds blocked their view, they would be able to see at a glance the natural geography and topography of the entire American Midwest—features which are also part of Indiana, and which have helped to give it, over the centuries, its special flavor and character.

They would be struck, first of all, by the intense greenness of the land. Agricultural crops predominate now, but Indiana was once part of a vast hardwood forest covering almost 90 percent of its thirty-six thousand square miles. Only 13 percent of that area is forested today, primarily in the southern half of the state, but also in the north, in the form of thousands of small woods and coppices scattered across the countryside.

These remain an important element of Indiana life. Just as the Englishman's character is said to be conditioned by the presence of the sea, never more than fifty miles away, the Hoosier is rarely out of sight of a sizeable stand of deciduous trees, reminders of the state's great woodland heritage.

Far to the east, where the primeval forest once began, the astronauts would also be able to see the long, wrinkled spine of the Appalachian mountains, the natural barrier which, shutting off the heartland from the east coast, determined more than any other geographic feature the manner in which Indiana was originally settled by persons of European descent. The Appalachians run northeast to southwest, from present-day Maine to Alabama, and their foothills extend into southern Ohio, eastern Kentucky, and southern Indiana. Much of the southern half of the Hoosier State is hilly, a fact which surprises casual visitors who have only traveled across the northern half and found it to be almost uniformly flat.

This difference is a legacy of the glaciers. They are gone now, of course, but the astronauts would be in a good position to study the terrain they were once drawn across, like vast white blinds, flattening everything beneath them. The fourth and last glacier, which leveled almost two-thirds of Indiana before receding ten thousand years ago, left the state divided into northern flatlands and southern hills and bestowed two other important gifts on the region.

Mile-thick layers of ice melting to the north formed the Great Lakes, orienting the state's northern tier to the watershed of the Saint Lawrence River and, ultimately, the Atlantic Ocean. Melted water rushing south carved out the Ohio River, the Wabash, and the latter's many tributaries, which fan out through most of

Indiana, all flowing in an opposite, southwesterly direction to the Mississippi River and the Gulf of Mexico. The geographic setting for Indiana's later importance as the crossroads of a continent had taken shape.

Prehistoric peoples had entered Indiana by the time the last glacier dwindled away. Archaeologists who have excavated their sites and examined their artifacts have pronounced them part of those larger midwestern cultures successively labeled Archaic, Woodland, and Mississippian. Through the centuries, as these early inhabitants developed tools, weapons, pottery, food-bearing plants, and forms of government, they also built enormous earthen mounds for burial and ceremonial purposes. These may be visited today throughout the state, most notably at the Mounds State Park in Anderson, the State Hospital in nearby New Castle, and the Angel Mounds Memorial near Evansville.

For reasons not yet understood, the people who established Angel Mounds and other late Mississippian settlements had either died out or gone elsewhere by 1500 A.D. The area from the Ohio River to the Lakes was essentially empty—a crossroads, but not a permanent home to any tribe. Some anthropologists believe Iroquois tribes from the east frightened the more peaceful Indians away from the area.

Whatever the cause, Indiana for the next three hundred years became the scene of a giant free-for-all, as a half dozen native tribes plus Spanish, French, British, and American forces entered the region and attempted to lay claim to it. It was time for recorded history to begin.

* * *

The Hoosier State. Heart of the Heartland. Smallest state west of the Alleghenies. Nineteenth state admitted to the Union. Most southern of the northern states.

John Dillinger robbed banks here, Dan Patch won harness races here, and Herb Shriner said that for something to do on Saturday nights back in his hometown they used to go down to the barbershop and watch haircuts. Oscar Robertson learned his basketball here. Cole Porter and Hoagy Carmichael tried out a few tunes on the piano in the parlor. As talented Hoosiers have always done, they all went off to the big city eventually. The processs continues. Recent Hoosier exports have dominated American popular music: singer Michael Jackson, country music star Janie Fricke, hard rocker John Cougar Mellencamp.

While all this is happening, Indiana remains what it has always been—home. At the heart of things. There is something strong and reassuring and at times even mysterious about the way it has continued to beat all these years, managing its own day-to-day affairs and at the same time sending its unique pulse out into the rest of the world.

Its statistics are simple: with 35,932 square miles, its land area places it thirty-eighth among the fifty states. It ranks twelfth in population, with about four and a half million people. In

Left to right: Circus City Festival, Peru. ■ Halftime performance during Indiana University football game. ■ Bust of Lew Wallace, author of *Ben-Hur,* Crawfordsville. ■

manufacturing it is eighth, in agricultural output, tenth. But these do not tell the whole story.

Indiana's true strength and staying power derive from the fact that it traditionally has been the "Crossroads of America." Location and geography gave it this role, and it has always been quick to experiment with new forms of transportation and communication, so that it remains a crossing-place, a connecting link.

Rivers and portages made the area a strategic part of the continent in pre-Revolutionary times, when the native tribe or European power controlling the old French forts at Lafayette, Fort Wayne, and Vincennes held the keys to traffic between the Great Lakes and the Mississippi River. By the time of the Civil War, roads, canals, and railroads had proliferated throughout the state, making Indianapolis, itself landlocked, the hub of a huge spoked wheel of transportation reaching halfway across the continent.

Still to come was the great boom in automobile manufacturing at the turn of the century, the brief but romantic love affair with the Interurban in the 1920s, the development of the Interstate Highway System in the period following World War II. And while the twentieth century was just beginning, a young Hoosier named Wilbur Wright moved with his family a few miles over the Ohio line to Dayton and with his brother Orville made the discoveries that would usher in the age of flight.

This fascination with movement and mobility is an inherent part of the Hoosier experience. The pioneers blazed their way into the wilderness carrying Kentucky longrifles and leading strings of pack animals. Initially, they came seeking land and an agricultural way of life, and rural values remain strong components in the state's makeup and outlook. But the need to get goods to market and to develop reliable forms of transportation led Hoosiers to begin making things with their hands—first wagons, then automobiles, then steel and basic metals, and so on, until the state became an important producer in the industrial age.

Traffic, then, is at the heart of what Indiana has been and is becoming. Sooner or later almost everybody and everything passes through the state, over it, or around a corner of it. This long-term experience has shaped the perceptions of both travelers and natives. The former, usually in a hurry, glimpse only a portion of the state and frequently claim it is "plain," or that there is a "sameness" about it. The latter, having viewed the changing procession from every angle, take a long view of things, and gradually develop a preference for that which is enduring and abiding.

There is a great deal of the permanent and the traditional in Indiana—just as there is an impressive range of scenery, from the dunes along Lake Michigan in the north to the woods and hills of Brown County in the south; from the farm towns in the central plains, with their endless acres of field corn and soybeans, to the old steamboat towns along the Ohio River, with their mossy warehouses and antebellum homes.

Indiana's people, too, exhibit this variety in a wealth of backgrounds and different racial and ethnic traditions. There is still a whisper of the Indian heritage in the names of towns like Kokomo, Loogootee, Mishawaka, and Winemac, lakes such as Tippecanoe and Maxinkuckee, rivers called the Wabash, the Mississinewa, the Salamonie. One can see French homes and buildings in Vincennes built long before the American Revolution, neat Quaker homesteads in the Whitewater region near Richmond, Amish buggies lined up in the yard of a plain white farmhouse north of Fort Wayne.

Indiana's cities show a similar diversity. Fort Wayne is the oldest and most traditional, with roots going back to Indian settlements and to French trading posts established in the late seventeenth century. South Bend came into prominence as a manufacturing center during the Civil War under the leadership of the Studebaker brothers. During the Civil War period, Evansville became a broker of traffic and goods on the Ohio River. Today, its manufacturing and industrial prowess make it the major southern Indiana city. On the shores of Lake Michigan, Gary began as a planned city in 1905 when it sprang from the forehead of its corporate parent, United States Steel. With its sister cities of Hammond, East Chicago, and Whiting, it has become an important steel-producing and petroleum-refining area. At the center of the state, Indianapolis offers one of the country's newest major art museums, a leading symphony orchestra, a professional theater, and the largest children's museum in the world.

Rather than extremes—of scenery, material possessions, or behavior—Indiana is a place where a great deal has been tried out, sifted through, experimented with. In short, it is an essentially democratic place, a middle ground, where things are encouraged to come together and find their own balance.

The Socialist Party was founded in Indianapolis; so was the John Birch Society. The United Mine Workers once had their headquarters in the city, and the American Legion's national offices are a few blocks north of the Circle. Out of such diversity of opinion and belief comes not uniformity but tolerance, a willingness to compromise, a respect for fair play.

Indiana's pulse is a variation on a familiar rhythm, an alternation between those timeless polarities of rural and urban, traditional and modern, then and now, which give character to a countryside or a civilization. In serious terms it is an honorable debate, a dialogue on the nature of life and government which goes back to Jefferson and Hamilton, Tecumseh and Harrison.

And in comic terms? The purest version, beloved by all Hoosiers, is the archetypal confrontation between the city slicker who, in his open-topped touring car, just passing through on his way to Chicago, has somehow managed to get lost a few miles south of Shelbyville, and the farmer, in straw hat and bib overalls, leaning against the fence and chewing on a blade of Timothy grass, who waits for the inevitable question.

* * *

In the fall, people in Indiana like to go to Brown County. It is traditional, like getting out in the front yard to rake the leaves, or carving a Halloween pumpkin. Some Hoosiers have been going to Brown County since they were children, when they were taken there by their parents. Brown County State Park is a favorite place for college students to spend an afternoon tramping in the woods, and in good weather visitors of all ages throng the streets of the little town of Nashville, the county seat.

Fall leaves, which Brown County has, in great and colorful profusion, do not really explain its popularity. Other counties have leaves too, and they become just as brilliant and eye-catching as the leaves in Brown County. Nor can the attraction be explained in terms of all those hills and high overlooks which hold, it is alleged, a strange fascination for Hoosiers and other midwesterners who live out in the flatlands. There are plenty of hills in Brown County, to be sure, and they are a joy to visit any time of the year, any season. But there are hills in other parts of Indiana, too. What, then, is Brown County's secret? Why is it that while only a few Hoosiers have ever gotten out and walked along the banks of the Wabash, a great many of them flock to Brown County every year?

In a word, Brown County is different. Different from anywhere else in Indiana, perhaps in the country. Exactly how it is different is left up to the individual. It offers something for everyone—scenery, outdoor activities, entertainment, restaurants, retail shops which sell everything from quality Hoosier crafts to expensive imported sportswear. In Brown County you can camp out or stay in a well-appointed motel. You can take the family or go by yourself and meet new people. It is a do-it-yourself sort of place, neighborly, and fun. It is worth visiting precisely because it provides such a contrast to the adjoining counties and to the rest of the state.

You first begin to realize what sort of place Brown County is by going there. It is located in the south-central portion of Indiana, and no matter from which direction you are coming, you will travel through a part of the state which is profoundly Hoosier, and, just as profoundly, not like Brown County at all.

Begin at Indianapolis, at the center of the state. Here are museums and skyscrapers, hotels and department stores, interstate highways, condominiums, shopping centers, an international airport, all features common to any large American city. A stronger sense of the city's character can be found in its many residential neighborhoods, some noted for their historical backgrounds, others for their homes, which are built in certain periods or styles. Typical among these are Irvington, Woodruff Place, Golden Hill, Ravenswood, and the Old Northside. Then there are towns along the edge of the metropolis, such as Beech Grove, Speedway, and Lawrence, which have elected to keep their own governments and have preserved their particular identities.

Indianapolis has brand-name factories which employ thousands of workers—Eli Lilly, Detroit Diesel Allison, Stokely-Van Camp, RCA, Chevrolet, International Harvester, Ford, and Chrysler. But as one drives south it also becomes apparent that the area's industrial base is broad and diversified, and made up of many smaller plants specializing in electronics, tool and die-making, plastics, metal-fabrication. Here, as elsewhere in the state, small factories are constantly starting up while others re-tool for new products, new procedures.

Indiana shares in the midwestern tradition which encourages the fledgling entrepreneur, the risk-taker, the tinkerer willing to try out a new idea. The spirit of Edison and the Wright brothers is strong here. It is the sort of place where an ambitious individual can take the plunge, get a loan from the local bank, set up a shop in an old roller-rink, hire a couple of young electrical engineers just out of Purdue, start producing some new health-care device or aerospace component, and in the process find out what the free-enterprise system is all about.

In Indianapolis in the early 1950s, a man named Howard Sams thought it might help electrical repairmen if they could consult diagrams of the circuits in the new television sets appearing on the market. He borrowed a few hundred dollars, quit his job, took apart some sets, and hired a draftsman to draw schematics of the wiring. Then he went out and sold them. The demand was so great that within a few years the Howard Sams Company had become one of the nation's major technical publishers, providing jobs for hundreds of Hoosiers, while Sams himself became a millionaire.

More recently, in the town of Mitchell, a metal-stamping plant receiving reduced orders from the automobile industry was about to go under. Plant officials decided to switch from stamping parts to building industrial robots, and their business turned around overnight. The work force returned and the plant teamed up with nearby Vincennes University to offer a robotics repair program. It was another frost-belt success story, one in which everybody involved came out ahead.

Where do such workers come from in Indiana? The big cities, surely, where most of the state's industry is concentrated. But also from the suburbs and farms. Almost a quarter of the Indianapolis work force commutes from outside of Marion County. Drive a bit farther south on your way to Brown County, and you'll think you are finally in the country. Leave Interstate 465 for old State Road 135, which is the best way to get to Brown County from the north, and the landscape looks like any other part of rural Indiana—level terrain, an occasional patch of woods where the stock can find shade in the summer, white frame farmhouses with outbuildings and barns, and lots of soybeans and corn.

Every once in a while the car passes a meadow where beef cattle are grazing, or dairy cows, and now and then a herd of sheep. But the most common farm animal here and elsewhere in the state is that ubiquitous and thoroughly contrary creature, the hog. It is said that in Indiana more corn goes to market on the hoof than by the bushel. This is true. Most of it goes in the form of thousands of carefully tended and scientifically fattened young pigs. Indiana, which has a state bird and state tree, has, as yet, no state animal. If a referendum were held, the hog would be the odds-on favorite.

To the rest of the nation, Indiana is a major supplier of pork and its related products. But the hog, important as a relatively quick cash producer, is seldom the sole source of income on Indiana's small farms. Many operators of these single-family farms in Johnson County work in factories in Indianapolis or Columbus. Their first love is farming, but most of them manage to make ends meet only by putting in eight hours a night at the local factory, then getting up the next morning to put in six or eight more hours driving a tractor. Few complain. Call it basic American perseverance or Hoosier contrariness, they make their own decisions and provide for their families by being both good workers and good farmers.

Like farmers and small landholders everywhere, such Hoosiers would like to see their children continue on the land. Yet at the same time, they have the typical American hope that their children will not have to work as hard as they do in order to make a living. Good schools can make the difference. The visitor who comes at Brown County from another direction will encounter one of the many institutions of higher education in which Hoosiers place a great deal of hope for the future. To approach Brown County from the west is to drive through Bloomington, the seat of Monroe County and the location of Indiana University, the state's largest liberal-arts school.

Hoosiers call it simply IU. Bordering downtown Bloomington, it has one of the most beautiful campuses in the country. Everywhere there are trees, gently rolling hills, meadows, and shady walkways leading past scores of buildings and dormitories made of native limestone. Over thirty thousand students study here, most of them majoring in the humanities. The University also offers first-rate schools of music, business, and law, and, at the Indianapolis campus, the largest medical school in the world, which graduates over five hundred new doctors each year.

Complementing these opportunities in public-supported education are those offered by IU's northern counterpart, Purdue University, in West Lafayette, where engineering, science, and agriculture are dominant along with programs in business, pharmacy, and veterinary science. The two other major public universities are Indiana State in Terre Haute, a training ground for teachers, and Ball State in Muncie, also known for its programs in education and for its recently chartered college of architecture and city planning.

These four state schools maintain regional campuses in several cities—Gary, Hammond, South Bend, Fort Wayne, Kokomo, Indianapolis, Richmond, Evansville, New Albany. To the programs offered in these locations may be added those of the state's fifth major university, Notre Dame, in South Bend, plus those

made available by the wealth of smaller universities and private colleges, including Hanover, Evansville, Franklin, Earlham, Butler, Indiana Central, Anderson, Wabash, DePauw, Saint Joseph's, and Tri-State. No matter where they might live in the state, Hoosiers seeking additional education can find an appropriate course of study within reasonable driving distance.

Rather than the ivy-covered buildings and Big Ten athletic facilities of Bloomington, the visitor approaching Brown County from the east encounters a world of surprising modernity and architectural grace in the city of Columbus in Bartholomew County. For many years the Cummins Engine Foundation, which is allied with the city's largest industry, has facilitated both the preservation of local historical landmarks and the design of impressive new contemporary structures. Over forty public, private, and industrial buildings here are the work of some of the best-known architects in the twentieth century — Eliel and Eero Saarinen, I. M. Pei, Cesar Pelli, and others. Sculptors Henry Moore, Jean Tinguely, and Robert Indiana are also represented in the public buildings and plazas Columbus offers to visitors and architecture students from around the world.

To come from the south, a final avenue of approach to Brown County, the visitor passes through the monumental evidence of an industry based on limestone, one of the state's most important natural resources. Bedford, in Lawrence County, is the capital of this industry. Ranged all around it are the steep-walled quarries which, over the years, have furnished high-quality stone for buildings everywhere in the United States. Here it is possible to stand on a high cliff and look down into an emptiness which years ago held the stone for the Empire State Building, or, more recently, the American United Life Building in Indianapolis.

Diversified industry, the nation's tenth largest university, one of the finest group of modern buildings in the Midwest, a major stone-quarrying region—these important parts of Indiana are quite different from anything to be found in Brown County. It prides itself on being traditionally Hoosier. It can be contrary, on occasion, but it is invariably laid back. If it specializes in anything at all, it is charm, which comes in assorted flavors. There are really several Brown Counties, and part of the pleasure of going there is finding the one which suits you.

There is, first, the Brown County which started it all—the old-time, backwoods, limestone chimney sort of world made up of homesteads and log cabins built by the first settlers. This world, carefully nourished today by shops and restaurants which partake of the tradition, perpetuates its authenticity with a great deal of humor and pride in a number of details and stories about the area, such as the place names of various trails through the hills, lookout points, and crossroad settlements.

Close to Nashville, the visitor may encounter Bear Wallow and Milk-Sick Bottoms. Whippoorwill Hollow and Scarce o' Fat Ridge are a bit harder to find. Farther out in the county are the little

communities of Gnawbone, Beanblossom, Dead Fall, and Stone Head. With a good map and local directions, you can still get to Possum Hollow or stop off for a visit to Stoney Lonesome, once regarded as the dreariest spot between Columbus and Nashville. Here, in earlier days, according to one guidebook, "robber bands ... lay in wait for any unsuspecting land-buyer or other trader ... carrying money upon his person."

Among the unsuspecting came artists, who began arriving in Brown County at the turn of the century in search of inexpensive housing and colorful landscapes. Between the wars they made Nashville into a pleasant summer art colony, rather like a land-locked Provincetown. It retains this atmosphere today. There are small museums, framing shops, and dozens of galleries. Paintings hang everywhere—in restaurants, in drugstores.

There have been all kinds of artists in Nashville, from Sunday painters to National Academicians. One of Indiana's best paint-ers, T. C. Steele, had a studio west of Nashville which is now maintained as a state memorial. After three-quarters of a century, the artists and craftspeople working in Nashville today have sto-ries and tales almost as audacious as those told by descendants of the original settlers. Take Onya La Tour, for example. A Hoosier, she went to New York in the 1920s and became acquainted with artists in the *Société Anonyme*, which was instrumental in the founding of the Museum of Modern Art. She supported herself and a daughter by modeling and working in galleries. Gradually, she acquired works by painters who were, in those days, mostly unknown—Jackson Pollock, Stuart Davis, Arthur Dove, and Moses Soyer. In 1940 she loaded five hundred of their paintings and sculptures in a truck and headed west.

She drove to a farmhouse east of Nashville and hung up some of her paintings, calling the collection the Indiana Museum for Modern Art, but no one paid much attention to her. She survived by working in a Columbus factory. After the war, she had little success in interesting Hoosiers in her paintings. Fortunately, a wealthy industrialist understood what she was trying to do. They married, and for the rest of her life spent summers in Nashville, displaying the art in their sumptuous hillside home. It has been said, in retrospect, that the truckload of paintings she drove from New York to Nashville in 1940 was the most important collection of modern works ever assembled in the American Midwest.

Literary Brown County has produced traditions and stories of its own. There are always writers in Nashville: James Whitcomb Riley's secretary and biographer, Marcus Dickey, was a longtime resident; Hoosier journalist Ernie Pyle spent time in Nashville and published a fine essay about it shortly before going off to cover World War II. More recently, Don Pendleton (a pseudonym), author of an extremely successful series of paperback thrillers, lived in Nashville for several years. Novelist James Alexander Thom lives in a cabin between Nashville and Bloomington. But the most prominent Nashville literary figure is that of Abe Martin,

the bewhiskered, crackerbox philosopher created by Indiana humorist Kin Hubbard.

Hubbard was a staff artist for the *Indianapolis News* when his first Abe Martin cartoon appeared in 1904. Abe lounges on a Brown County streetcorner observing the passing scene in a laconic, homespun dialect which, when syndicated in three hun-dred newspapers, soon had the entire nation laughing. "A loafer must feel funny when a holiday comes along," Abe observes, making fun of himself and all other practitioners of the art. "A loafer allus has a nickel plated pencil holder."

Hubbard peopled Nashville with dozens of imaginary neigh-bors — the artsy Miss Fawn Lippincut, the Hon. Ex-Editor Cale Fluhart, and Mrs. Germ Williams, who made a fortune in the poultry business. One of his favorite targets was civic booster Tell Binkley, who, Abe announced one day, "has quit work an' accepted a position." Hubbard parodied the personal columns of the small-town newspaper and read the society pages carefully: "There was a ole fashioned one-ring weddin' at th' Tiford Moots home t'day," he reported, adding that "some folks git credit fer havin' hoss sense that hain't ever had enough money t' make fools o' themselves."

This was country humor in the grand American tradition of Artemus Ward, Josh Billings, and Mark Twain. Hubbard immedi-ately became the peer of two other well-known Hoosier humor-ists, James Whitcomb Riley and George Ade. Later he struck up friendships with Will Rogers and Franklin P. Adams. His *Abe Martin* books made him a wealthy man, but he chose to remain in Indianapolis and avoid the limelight. "I've had a couple of chances to go to New York and make something of myself," he acknowledged, "but I'd rather stay here where I can get in the band."

Eighty-odd years later, his reputation as a classic American humorist has not dimmed. With an intentional artlessness he slipped past the reader's assumptions about rural life in order to accomplish the serious work of satire and social commentary. He was also an acute observer of the national scene: "Ther's some folks standin' behind the president," he declared, "that ought t' git around where he kin watch 'em."

* * *

There are, besides Brown County, ninety-one other counties in Indiana and they are named after everything from Revolutionary War heroes (Fayette, Green, Kosciusko, Pulaski), to once-promi-nent Indian peoples (Delaware, Elkhart, Miami). Marion County, where Indianapolis is located, was originally so sodden and infested by mosquitoes that its settlers named it in honor of Fran-ces Marion, the Revolutionary War general whose nickname was "The Swamp Fox."

With 671 square miles, Allen is the biggest Indiana county. Its county seat is Fort Wayne, which has a metropolitan-area popu-lation of 380,000 persons. While many native and European

Left to right: Dancers with Indianapolis Ballet Theatre. ■ Amish children near Fort Wayne. ■ Crooked Lake, west of Pokagon State Park. ■ Conner Prairie Pioneer Settlement, Noblesville. ■

traditions came together to form Fort Wayne, the greatest number of immigrants were Germans, both Lutherans and Catholics. The smallest Indiana county, with just 5,000 people, is Ohio, on the southeastern border. Rising Sun, its county seat, is one of the historic old steamboat towns on the Indiana side of the Ohio River. During early territorial days, there was only one county, Knox, "the mother of counties." Its capital was Vincennes and it comprised what eventually became the state in 1816. Several Indiana counties located along the Ohio River — Posey, Warrick, Perry, Harrison, and Clark — were carved out of Knox.

Just as the capital of the territory and the state was located in three different places between 1801 and 1825 — first Vincennes, then Corydon, finally Indianapolis — county seats also shifted, while surveying and the establishing of boundary lines continued. Merom, a beautiful old river town on bluffs high above the Wabash River, between Vincennes and Terre Haute, was once the county seat of Sullivan County, but by 1842 a coal-mining boom farther inland required the county government to move to the newly platted town of Sullivan, some ten miles east. It was an orderly removal, though such transfers of power did not always go so smoothly.

On the opposite side of the state, in Wayne County, the county seat of Centerville prospered from its dealings with pioneers heading west along the National Road and prided itself on having produced two of Indiana's most illustrious statesmen of the Civil War era. Local attorney Oliver P. Morton became the state's wartime "iron governor" who saw to it that Indiana raised, on a per capita basis, more troops and money for the Northern cause than any other state except Maine. But Centerville was also the home of George Washington Julian, Morton's arch political rival and for many years Indiana's chief liberal spokesman. Antislavery, women's suffrage, homesteading — Julian championed these and many other causes long before they were popular and paid a price. For advocating radical reconstruction of the South after the war, he was attacked and beaten in the Richmond, Indiana railroad station, and once a courtroom opponent cut his throat.

Both men were lawyers and both were mugwumps, which means they jumped party lines. Morton began as a Democrat and became a Republican; Julian, a Republican most of his life, turned Democrat in his old age. As idealistic young men in the 1850s, both had a great deal to do with the founding of the national Republican Party. For most of their political careers they conducted a vigorous debate, like the earlier Hamilton and Jefferson, on the merits of a strong central government versus the rights of the people.

With such stalwarts coming from Centerville, it might have seemed this was not a town to trifle with, but neither Morton nor Julian was present on that August day in 1873 when representatives of the even more prosperous village of Richmond, ten miles to the east, appeared in force and demanded the county records

be turned over to them. Centervillians barricaded themselves in the brick jailhouse; only when the attackers began firing on the building did they give in.

Richmond became, in time, a sizeable Indiana city and the center of commerce and industry in the region already known as the Whitewater district, after the river which, unlike all other rivers in central and southern Indiana, does not flow southwesterly toward the Wabash, but southeasterly toward the Ohio. A minor distinction, perhaps, but it may account for the fact that citizens in the Whitewater have always seen things from a slightly different perspective than other Hoosiers.

This first became evident in the 1820s when the area began filling up with Quaker farmers from the Carolinas who were completely opposed to slavery. By the 1840s they were doing a brisk business on the Underground Railroad, had established a number of important schools—one of which became Earlham College—and had contributed to the beginnings of a distinct Whitewater culture. Brookville, another important Whitewater town farther south, in Franklin County, had already sent a number of its attorneys to high political office in Indianapolis and Washington. In the 1830s, the National Road brought fresh ideas and new people to the area, and in the 1840s, the Whitewater Canal repeated this process. With a firm social, economic, and political base, the area was soon able to establish and support its own forms of art.

First among Whitewater artifacts which would receive critical acclaim from twentieth century art historians were the woven coverlets produced on jacquard looms by immigrant weavers prior to the Civil War. These craftsmen, who had been displaced by industrialization in England and Germany, created geometric, two-color coverlets, which constitute a significant contribution to nineteenth century American design.

The Whitewater area produced writers: novelist Lew Wallace was born in Brookfield, and noted ethnologist James Mooney came from Richmond. It also nourished a school of landscape painters known as the Richmond group, but its most enduring art came from a family of reclusive, self-effacing sisters named Overbeck, who founded an art pottery in Cambridge City in 1911 and supported themselves with its proceeds for the next forty-four years. Theirs is one of the major achievements in American design during the period between the wars.

There were six Overbeck sisters, born between 1862 and 1888 in the same farmhouse where they were to live and work most of their lives. Intelligent, introspective, shy, they became linked, through their early interest in china painting, with the ideals of the Arts and Crafts movement of the late nineteenth century. Reacting to the abuses of the industrial age, English craftsman William Morris and his followers insisted that everyone is a potential artist, that everything in the home — pottery, textiles, furniture — should be handmade, and that such objects must be at once simple, beautiful, and functional. The Overbeck sisters devoted their lives to this vision.

In a photograph taken when they were in their twenties and early thirties, they pose in a single row, all dressed in white, high-necked Victorian blouses, all but one wearing gold-rimmed glasses, all with the same high foreheads and pensive mouths. Only Margaret, the oldest, is smiling. It was her idea to start the pottery, and she would die in the same year the dream was realized. The others carried on, and in the years that followed each became a specialist: Hannah was the designer, the observer of nature; Elizabeth, the master potter; Mary, the youngest, best at decorating the wares. Harriet, musician and linguist, kept house for the others and read aloud to them as they worked. Ida, the only sister to marry, returned home again after her husband died.

It was a remarkable household. "They lived unto themselves," one scholar observed, "with commitment only to themselves and their drive to create." They produced one-of-a-kind ceramic vases and objects which, in chronological terms, followed art nouveau and preceded art deco; in artistic terms, what they did was intentionally American and wholly original. The Overbeck sisters were not interested in assembly-line methods or in imitating European or Oriental models. "If anything characteristic or original is to be accomplished," Elizabeth wrote in her journal, "it is necessary to begin at the beginning and build up the foundation for oneself." Everything she and her sisters strove to achieve could be summed up in two basic principles: "All good applied design is original" and "All borrowed art is dead art."

Tough words. But then, these sisters all grew up on a farm in Indiana.

* * *

Hoosiers are inordinately fond of tall tales, but there is not much left for them to exaggerate when the discussion comes around to the subject of the annual 500-Mile Race at Indianapolis. It has become, over the years, one of the most spectacular and exciting sporting events in the world.

Now approaching its seventieth running, the Indianapolis 500 attracts the same sort of international attention as the Olympic Festival or the World Cup Soccer Tournament. It is clearly the best-known American sporting event. Most Europeans, Africans, Asians, and Australians are only mildly interested in the outcome of the World Series or the Superbowl. But travel virtually anywhere abroad, let it be known that you are from Indiana, and immediately you will be welcomed—and questioned minutely—by some race fan who has listened to radio broadcasts of the Race for years and will be dazzled to hear that you once had a pass to walk around in the pits, knew someone on Bobby Unser's crew, or shook hands with Janet Guthrie.

It is not hard to do any of these things in Indiana, especially if you live in the central part of the state. As soon as basketball season ends with the high-school finals on the last Saturday in March, a Hoosier's thoughts turn not to springtime but to racetime. By early April the first few cars begin venturing, unofficially, out on the track, and the sportswriters start tuning up their superlatives. In May, the Race takes over: there are charity balls and media interviews, a mayor's breakfast and a pageant of princesses, a golf tournament and a mini-marathon, all capped by a nationally televised parade through downtown Indianapolis complete with flower-bedecked floats, antique cars, marching bands, and celebrities from television and professional sports. This is Indiana's equivalent of the Mardi Gras or the Rose Festival, but the true Hoosier race fan is careful not to let any of it interfere with two much older rituals—going out to the time trials, and getting a good parking place in the infield on race day.

On two qualifying weekends preceding the Race, eighty or ninety cars compete for the fastest four-lap time around the two-and-a-half-mile oval and a place among the thirty-three starting positions. Monday through Friday, the drivers take practice laps while the technicians and mechanics tinker with the backup cars. For many Hoosiers, going out to the track to watch either the practicing or the qualifying runs is the most enjoyable part of the entire month.

On qualification days, one sits almost anywhere among the acres of permanent bleachers and stands with a portable radio and a Styrofoam cooler at hand, soaking up a bit of sun, listening to the different times being announced over the loudspeakers, and cheering one's favorite drivers as they roar down the straightaway. In the pits, crew members swarm around the cars when they pull off the main track for repairs or adjustments. Exact attendance figures are never released by the race authorities, but if the weather is good, time-trial crowds estimated to be in excess of one hundred thousand are not unusual.

Even on weekdays the temptation of "bugging out" to the track on a warm May afternoon empties out half of the student populations in high schools on the west side of Indianapolis and creates serious absentee problems everywhere else, from factories to nursing homes. Those who can't make it to the track are busy back at the shop or the office drawing up pools—pick your favorite driver for a dollar, collect fifteen or twenty if he (or she) comes in among the first three places.

Originally run on Memorial Day, the Race now starts at 11 A.M. on the Sunday prior to the "official" Monday holiday, which also serves as a rain date, though it has seldom been necessary. The weather is uncommonly temperate and fair during late May in Indiana, and festivities surrounding the 500 are as much a celebration of the coming of summer as they are of automobile-racing skill and daring.

During the three-day weekend, many Hoosiers plan informal family reunions or get-togethers with friends. Some stage elaborate patio parties complete with checkered-flag decorations and racing-car insignia. Others participate in the weekend's excitement simply by turning on the radio during the running of the race, while they wash the family car or work in the garden.

Older traditions are remembered, too, since it is still Decoration Day for many people. Sometime during the weekend one usually arranges to drive a grandmother or a widowed aunt out to the local cemetery to spruce things up around the family plots and perhaps to leave fresh-cut peonies on the headstones, or small American flags stuck in the earth on each veteran's grave.

Whatever else happens, the evening before the race is definitely party time. On the previous evening the festival princesses and their escorts and all the parade celebrities and track officials and media people danced the night away. Now even if one is not involved in a full-scale Race party, it is still time to get the grill out of the garage, put on a few steaks or hamburgers, ice down the cooler, invite the next-door neighbors over, and speculate whether some new lead-footed rookie fresh from the midgets and sprint tracks is going to rewrite all the record books.

If there are older teenagers in the family, they may have left for the Speedway already, intent on becoming a part of the impromptu, all-night carnival ranging up and down Sixteenth Street, north of the track. This gathering, which greatly vexes law-enforcement authorities, is not for the faint of heart. Crowds overflow from taverns and nightspots in the track's westside vicinity, moiling about and looking for action. It is routine to see motorcycle gangs from around the country weaving through the bunched-up cars. But these wandering bands of merrymakers and occasional rowdies are mere prelude to the hoardes that have already begun to assemble in lines fanning back from each of the Speedway's twelve gates, rather like pioneers waiting for the pistol shot that will start the great land rush.

The 500-Mile Race draws the largest paying crowd for a single-day sporting event in the world—around 325,000 people. Of these, some 236,000 will have purchased tickets for reserved seats in the grandstands and permanent bleachers. That leaves approximately 90,000 additional fans who prefer to drive their cars or trucks inside the track and park them in designated sections of the 224-acre infield on a first-come, first-served basis. The gates open at 5 A.M., a few minutes before sunrise. Those who manage to get close to the fences will be able, six hours later, to watch most of the Race from their vehicles.

Lines made up of those hoping to get good spots in the infield begin forming the night before the Race. There are always a few who have waited in their campers for days or even weeks. For these loyalists, the only way to see the Race is from the infield. All those people sitting in their fancy, air-conditioned, glassed-in suites on top of the southwest turn are missing the point: you don't watch the Race, you experience it.

When the pace car pulls over and the Race actually begins, you can't hear anything anyway—the roar of the engines is astoundingly loud, all-pervasive, and, for the next few hours, inescapa-

ble. Nor is it easy to leave the track, should you be so inclined. Traffic everywhere is impenetrable: you are there for the duration.

The Race is never televised live. If you want to see it, you have to attend, regardless of the risks or difficulties. The fans in the infield are lucky to have their cars along, in case the going gets tough. An infield ticket is also the cheapest possible way to get inside the track to see the Race. But the real reason why thousands head faithfully for the infield each year derives from the history of the Race itself.

In the 1920s and 30s, poor roads and frequent flat tires made the drive to Indianapolis from other towns throughout the state or adjoining states a major excursion. The Race itself took six hours to run back then. (Today it requires less than three.) Fast foods were unheard of, and concessions at the track were minimal. Accurate weather prediction was still in its infancy. As a matter of course, anyone setting out to watch the entire Race took along a trunk full of food, water, picnic supplies, even bedding and tents. It was rather like going on safari.

Many of today's fans first saw the Race from the infield when they were brought there by their parents, twenty or thirty years ago, as part of this informal expeditionary army. There is really no need for such elaborate preparations today, but the infield is still a place for roughing it—for showing up with enough gear to sit through any conceivable sort of weather or procedural delay. It also accommodates those last-minute fans who, sitting in a bar in Jeffersonville or Hobart on Saturday evening, suddenly decide to drive to the Race the next day. They may not have advance tickets, but they know they can always squeeze into the infield.

The infield is wild and unpredictable. Its most notorious section is "The Snake Pit," on the inside of the southwest turn, where young people like to gather before and during the Race. For these and many others, the challenge of returning to the infield year after year is irresistible. After waiting in line the entire night, there is still nothing quite like surging through the gates with thousands of other vehicles, bouncing across the ruts and the gullies, finally pulling in at the right place, and then, just as the dust settles and the rising sun brings everything out of the shadows, getting out for a look around.

What one sees, in all directions, is the world as parking lot: cars, trucks, vans, motorcycles, pickups, campers, an occasional old yellow schoolbus or fire engine or reconditioned Greyhound, all of them drawn up in ranks facing the track, a great vast sea of them, as though the vehicles themselves were sentient and had flocked here, like some migrating species, to watch their faster, sleeker brethren perform this annual ritual essential to the well-being of all.

The Race celebrates one of the twentieth century's most durable, important, and troubling inventions, the automobile. To the infield crowd it would be unthinkable to hold such rites and not bring along one's own car or truck. This dimension of the Race is

invisible to the millions listening to it on the radio, or seeing it later on television reruns, or reading about it in the press, but it is at the heart of Race mystique. Veteran infielders can even remember a golden age when their vehicles enabled them to overcome the one disadvantage of being in the infield—a time when they actually had some of the best seats at the track.

The ticket holders in the stands have one clear advantage: they are sitting in raked rows, above the action, and can look out and down at the cars as they flash by. Latecomers parked ten or twelve rows deep in the infield can see nothing at all except each other. Even so, for a few brief, glorious years back in the 1950s, Hoosier ingenuity and infield know-how managed to surmount this drawback. Infield patrons simply brought along enough building materials and assorted scaffolding to construct their own viewing stands on the tops of their cars and trucks, or next to them. My earliest recollections of the Race date from this strange and nearly forgotten era of infield craziness.

My father was a teenager when he first attended the Race in the 1920s with his father. My grandfather Carter was a general contractor who drove a horse and wagon until 1920, when he traded in the rig for his first International truck. One of the first places he went in his newfangled invention was to the Race. By the time I was old enough to attend the Race in the late 1940s, the drive down had become an annual family ritual.

Although my mother had no interest in going, for days before the Race she would fix large quantities of fried chicken and potato salad and bread-and-butter sandwiches. Other provisions—iced tea, soft drinks, suntan lotion, coolers, containers of water—were carefully laid by. We set out at one or two in the morning to make the forty-mile trip to Indianapolis. There might be four grown-ups crowded into the pickup's cab — my father, an uncle or two, perhaps a neighbor—and a half dozen small boys clinging to the baskets and lawn chairs and lumber in the bed of the truck. My older brother and I and two cousins regularly attended, and we usually invited other schoolfriends to go with us. It was an unspeakably exciting journey.

We were out in the dark and the elements, wrapped in blankets and hunched down against the wind. The world—what we could see of it by the dim light of streetlamps and advertising signs — dwindled away behind us. As we neared the track and slowed down to enter the streams of traffic gathering there, our excitement was complete. We might, if we were lucky, glimpse a few race cars whizzing along later that morning. But we were already caught up in something inherently satisfying because it was so unbelievably big and vast.

My father's favorite place to park was the northeast turn. Our pickup truck had a welded-pipe rack projecting above the bed. It was a simple matter to lay a deck of two-by-sixes on this rack, hand up the lawn chairs, and find oneself on a perfect observation platform from which to look out over the other cars and trucks and see the Race. All around us people with similar trucks were doing the same. During the next few years all of us made improvements and brought in more building materials. What we once threw up in a few minutes now took several hours to construct, and we worked diligently to have our towers in place by the time the Race began.

Hoosiers are an enterprising people. By 1955 the infield along the northeast turn was filled with a hundred of these oddball platforms and leaning towers. Some were freestanding, others sprouted from the beds of trucks used for hauling cattle or heavy machinery. Additional tiers went up from the base level, with decks supplied for each tier. The entrepreneurs who built them charged the groundlings a dime to sit on the first level, a quarter for the next, and so on up to the dollar seats, which swayed in the breeze but afforded a marvelous view of the track.

By the late 1950s our family's tower went up four tiers from the bed of our pickup, or about twenty feet, and, like all the other towers that high, had to be held in place by ropes guyed to the truck's fenders and an occasional two-by-four stake hammered into the ground. My father, a builder all his life, took great care to insure that the structure was safe. Still, at the top, when the wind blew and the ropes hummed with shifting tensions, I fancied it was the closest one could get to sailing without actually being out on the water. It was strangely joyous and liberating to be simultaneously part of a crowd of a quarter of a million people, and yet to be above the earth, isolated, floating along.

By 1960, the construction of infield towers reached its greatest pitch—hundreds of them thrust up around the inside curves and straightaways. Many had grown to considerable heights and proportions. On the northwest turn one structure in particular went up seven scaffolding units — about as high as the roof of a two-story house — and had enough plank seats to hold a hundred spectators. This monster tower was guyed to the two-and-a-half-ton flatbed truck on which its builders had brought in the necessary scaffolding and lumber.

The Race that year featured a number of great competitors. On the pole was Eddie Sachs, one of the most personable and popular drivers ever to race at the brickyard. Joining him in the front row were Jim Rathmann and Roger Ward. The entire field got off to a good start and headed out into the pace lap. When thirty-three brightly colored cars in close formation came roaring around the southeast curve and into view on the back straightaway, excited fans on the big tower on the northeast curve moved instinctively toward the front of the scaffolding for a better view. The sudden weight shift punched the tower's steel legs down through its base of planks. The entire scaffolding "fell lazily forward," a newspaper account said later, "as screaming spectators ran frantically to escape falling timbers and bodies."

"It looked like the Hindenberg going down," my father said. "It seemed to take forever, and there were people letting go and

Left to right: Sledder masked against winter cold. ■ Bill Monroe performs during his annual bluegrass festival at Beanblossom. ■ Indianapolis home of Benjamin Harrison, twenty-third President of the United States. ■ Poetry reading during Riley Days Festival, Greenfield. ■

dropping away from it like flies." The tower fell across the fence where people were already crowded so closely they could not get out of the way. Two men were killed outright; eighty-four persons were injured. Rescuers and first-aid teams churned about pulling survivors from the mud and debris. "There was beer and fried chicken all over the place," one news photographer said. The Race went right on and was won eventually by Rathmann. None of the drivers and few of the onlookers knew about the tower accident until they saw the next day's news.

It was the worst spectator mishap in Speedway history. Scaffoldings were completely banned the following year and have never been allowed to return. It was, rightly, the end of an era. Most young people who follow the Race know that something terrible happened to one of those towers people used to build in the infield back in the 1950s, but the details are vague.

In 1964 I remember listening to the start of the Race on a borrowed transistor radio while staying in a youth hostel in Venice. On the third lap a rookie lost it coming out of the last turn, smacked the wall, and exploded in a ball of flame in the middle of the track. Right behind him came Eddie Sachs, who had nowhere to go. If he swerved right or left, he risked stacking up the veteran drivers bunched in back of him. Sachs had only a fraction of a second to decide. He took the burning car broadside. He and its driver became the fifty-fifth and fifty-sixth competitors to die at Indianapolis. I did not listen to the rest of the Race.

Twelve years later, when I went again, I sat in the stands, and it was not the same. For me, and probably for many others who were there, those days in the infield are well on their way to becoming just another story Hoosiers like to tell. But when we say we know a tall story about the Race, we are not exaggerating.

*　　*　　*

Small towns are important in Indiana: towns with names like Shoals, Tipton, Winchester, and Martinsville. Little towns where almost everybody can still trace his ancestry back to the Italians who came over to work on the railroad, or the Irish who were shipped in to dig the canal, or the Welsh who were needed to run the tinplate mill. If Ohio is a state composed of many cities, Indiana is a state made up of many small towns: Goshen, Attica, Boonville, Paoli.

Hoosiers debate among themselves about the nature and virtues of small-town life. Some argue that the classic small town of the 1920s and 30s is gone, that under pressure from television advertising and mass merchandising, shopping malls and franchised food chains, the older Hoosier culture has withered away. Thanks to the automobile, everything is close to everything else now. The result may be that "all of Indiana is suburb to Indianapolis."

Opposed to this is the view that the small town is alive and well. Or, an argument that cuts both ways, that there really are not any cities in Indiana, only a handful of overgrown towns. They

may be big in population — Indianapolis claims over a million in its metropolitan area, and there are ten other major urban areas in the state—but they are essentially small-town in outlook, behavior, and feel.

In these discussions the taxpayer, county editor, and state legislator are regularly heard from, but it is the mayor or the city manager on whose desk most of the problems of the state's cities and towns come to rest. Hoosiers expect their municipal officials to be neighborly and accessible, and most of them are. Whether you live in a large town or a small one, sooner or later you will find yourself talking to the mayor. Not necessarily because you have a problem to discuss, but because you keep running into him—or her—at the supermarket, the Kiwanis Club pancake supper, or the ball game.

At a faculty party in West Lafayette not long ago, the cordial, articulate woman in a dark suit who might have been the visiting economics lecturer was, in fact, the mayor of West Lafayette. In Indianapolis recently, as I headed east on Market Street, I noticed an extremely tall man walking along ahead of me. I am over six feet myself, and since I'm a Hoosier, my first reaction on seeing anyone taller than I am is to think about how I would go about guarding him in a basketball game. When we stopped for the traffic light, I recognized Mayor William Hudnut, and as we went on down the street we ended up talking not about basketball or even politics, supposedly the two subjects most dear to the hearts of all Hoosiers, but about literature, which is sometimes thought to run a close third.

Hudnut, a Princeton graduate and a Presbyterian minister, is typical of mayors in Indiana who are frequently leading citizens in the community before being called to office. Many go from city hall to higher office. Richard Lugar, a businessman and former Rhodes scholar, came to prominence as a member of the Indianapolis school board, was elected mayor in 1968, served for two terms, and then entered the United States Senate. Before he became a senator, Vance Hartke was billed admiringly as "the boy mayor of Evansville." Others establish national reputations while still in city hall—Gary's Richard Hatcher, for example, who is one of the country's most respected black leaders.

These are impressive names, but in thinking of Indiana one must keep in mind the little-known heroes and heroines of mayordom—the small-town mayors across the state who seldom attract much attention, who head their party's ticket and hold office for a term or two and then go back to their regular jobs.

In Elwood, one of these citizen politicians after World War II was Elmo Gustin. To the kids playing along the sidewalk he was serious and dignified, with gray hair and gold-rimmed glasses, but he always had time to speak to them. His term coincided with that of another midwesterner, Harry Truman, who also took pleasure in a brisk walk every morning. Truman had been a haberdasher; Elmo Gustin was a clothier by trade, manager of the leading men's

27

store in town. Though they never met, they were two of a kind— average Americans who answered the call to duty.

Elmo Gustin did an honest, competent job of running his hometown for a few years and presided over the Elwood Centennial, which was celebrated in 1952. In Indiana, centennial and bicentennial observances are popular occasions. All the men in town grow elaborate mustaches and beards, the women wear granny dresses and bonnets, and the children generally run about whooping and hollering and pretending to be Indians. A week in the summer is set aside for historical programs, picnics, and early forms of entertainment such as square-dancing and old-time fiddling contests.

In a community of twelve thousand souls, where most people know each other by name, Elmo Gustin had a considerable reputation as a singer. Members of a church choir in a small town usually do not have trained voices and make no special claims for their musical abilities. Most of them participated in high-school choir and continue to sing in church because they like music and enjoy the fellowship. Since they do not always have a special number ready for Sunday morning services, choir directors cultivate certain soloists around town who can fill in on short notice. Elmo Gustin was that kind of singer and he was also that important member of any small-town singing group—a bass who could make himself heard.

Sunday mornings, the mayor essayed seldom-heard inspirational numbers for basso, all of which featured nautical or military themes. The repertoire included such perennials as "Asleep in the Deep" and "When the Bell in the Lighthouse Rings, Ding-Dong." Sometimes the entire congregation, sensing that the mayor had been up half the night arguing with the zoning board and not really gotten off under a full head of steam that morning, began pulling for him as he labored like some thick, indomitable switch engine, huffing and puffing his way down the scale to descend finally upon that unbelievable, solemnly resonating G below C below middle C.

The typical small-town mayor in Indiana operates not only by precept and party principle but also on the basis of personal integrity and forcefulness. Two particularly admirable Hoosier mayors, George Dale of Muncie and Clare Bangs of Huntington, had an ability to pour sand on the rails and get down to business when the grade ahead seemed impossibly steep. They were also capable of tootling the whistle and laying on the steam when everybody else wanted to jump the cab.

Events during the 1920s and 30s got both of these Hoosiers into hot water — that happens to every mayor in Indiana and comes with the territory — but they got themselves out of it with a great deal of personal courage and nerve. They do not show up much in the history books, but in the towns where they held office, they are still very much remembered by the people.

The best account of George Dale's administration is given,

curiously, in two works of social anthropology, perhaps the best and most famous ever written — *Middletown*, which appeared in 1929, and its sequel, *Middletown in Transition*, published in 1937. They deal with nothing less than an across-the-board examination of the nature of the American urban community: wage-earning, homemaking, education, religion, and public affairs. They were based on exhaustive field work and interviews conducted in Muncie during the 1920s and 30s by the husband-and-wife team of Robert S. and Helen M. Lynd. To this day they remain classics in their field.

Robert Lynd, a Hoosier from New Albany who graduated from Princeton in 1914, met Helen Merrell, another midwesterner, while they were graduate students in sociology at Columbia University. They were preceded at Columbia by another famous husband-and-wife team of writers from Indiana—Charles and Mary Ritter Beard, he an economic historian from Knightstown, she a social theorist and feminist from Indianapolis. By the early 1920s, the Lynds had come to Indiana to conduct their monumental investigation into all areas of daily life in Muncie, which they had selected as a typical American city and which they called "Middletown" in their studies.

In an extensive footnote which sums up Muncie's mayor, George Dale, and his era in Indiana, they describe him as the "'white-haired little man with the seat worn out of his pants' who for twenty years had edited a local Democratic weekly. Always fearless, he rose to national prominence when, almost single-handed, he fought the Ku Klux Klan which ruled the state and city in the mid-1920s."

As Hoosiers began to get fed up with white-sheeted foolishness, "The tide turned against the Klan in the state and other papers began to widen the breaches begun by Dale." Klan leaders were exposed and convicted and Klan-supported politicians of both parties disgraced and turned out of office. The daily press was in the forefront of this battle, and when in 1928 the *Indianapolis Times* received a Pulitzer Prize for its leadership in fighting the Klan, it was an award of which courageous editors and reporters throughout Indiana could be proud.

But such contrariness was not at all scarce in Indiana during the Depression. At about the same time as George Dale was stirring things up in Muncie, his fellow mayor Clare Bangs, a few counties up the road, was standing the town of Huntington on its head. While no renowned sociologists applauded his deeds, he managed to attract national attention to his struggle against a major power company by becoming one of the few mayors in American history to conduct town affairs while locked up in the county jail. This Bangs accomplished, for 101 days, with considerable verve and wit, to the consternation of his opponents and the delight of his constituents.

January of 1935 was the bottom of the Depression. The Democrats had recently come to power but their proposals for change had not yet taken effect, and there was considerable suffering and disillusionment across the country. In Huntington, the Northern Indiana Power Company was shutting off the electricity of townspeople who were behind in paying their bills.

The city of Huntington had a pair of Diesel-electric generators in city hall which furnished power for street lights and municipal buildings. Upon being sworn in, one of the mayor's first acts was to run city utility lines out to the homes of citizens left sitting in the dark by the power company. The firm's lawyers quickly obtained a restraining order to prevent further hookups, followed by an injunction to keep Huntington out of the commercial power business. Six days after taking office, to avoid being served with the relevant papers, Bangs went underground.

He continued to run the city of Huntington by means of "secret operations" and mysterious telephone calls for the next few months. The *Huntington Herald-Press* reported that he met with the board of works "in an automobile one night last week." Ten members of his administration were co-defendants in civil suits filed by the power company, and most of the townspeople were behind him.

Light crews in Huntington continued to string lines to private homes, while Bangs stayed in hiding, appearing unpredictably in nearby towns to chat with reporters and poke fun at Northern Indiana Power and its machinations. When he came out of hiding in April to appear before a judge, he was found to be in civil contempt of the power company's injunction and ordered to pay $1,500 damages and post a $2,000 bond. He refused, citing a 1931 Indiana statute providing that municipal officers may appeal from court judgments without posting bond. When this appeal was denied, he turned himself in at the county jail.

There he remained for the next 101 days, running the affairs of the town, conducting city council meetings in his cell, playing checkers, posing for pictures, and shrewdly attracting national and even international attention for his cause. The Indiana Supreme Court freed him on August 18, and Northern Indiana Power completely withdrew from the town, leaving Public Service of Indiana to come in and offer both lower rates and more flexible credit. David had beaten Goliath. Robin Hood had tweaked the Sheriff of Nottingham's nose. Or, to put it in Hoosier terms, another Indiana mayor had shown, when the going got tough, just how contrary he could really be.

*   *   *

How do Hoosiers sound when they talk? There is a Hoosier accent, surely, and to the outsider it can seem suspiciously Southern, but this is due more to its rhythms and trace words than its pronunciation or tone. The way Hoosiers speak English depends to a considerable extent on patterns developed in the eighteenth and early nineteenth centuries in western Virginia and the Carolina uplands. These areas provided the greatest number of pioneers who came over the mountains to the Ohio River Valley seeking new land in Kentucky and southern Indiana.

The way many Hoosiers talk today is full of words which show this kinship. They still use a "skillet" for fixing breakfast, see a "snake feeder" hovering on the waters of the "crick," and are likely to have "roasting ears" for dinner. All of these terms have Southern origins. Yet there are boundary lines within the state. North of Indianapolis, on the way to Fort Wayne, one will probably hear the bone from a chicken's breast called a "wishbone." Below Indianapolis, it is more likely to be called a "pullybone."

In general, the farther north one travels in Indiana, the more people begin to sound like people living in Detroit or Chicago; the farther south, the more like Louisville or Paducah. In between, the typical Hoosier will still put an "r" in the first syllable of "Washington" and say "whenever" when he means simply "when." For the most part it's "bucket" rather than "pail," but "bag" rather than "sack" or "poke."

Sometime during the early years of statehood the Southern tradition began to blend with a more distinct, Yankee way of speaking—yet another instance of the state's two waves of immigration flowing together to form the distinctively Hoosier. Two important Indiana writers demonstrated the results of this blending.

First published in 1871, Edward Eggleston's *The Hoosier Schoolmaster* depicted life on the southern Indiana frontier by dramatizing a young teacher's struggle to teach "good" English to his students and to demonstrate fair play to an entire community. Teachers have always faced such tasks, but Eggleston's book is of particular interest today for the curious manglings of grammar and syntax purportedly common among unlettered Hoosiers of the pre-Civil War period.

Eggleston listened to this Hoosier talk and wrote it down in a quasi-phonetic way. "It takes a right smart man to be a schoolmaster in Flat Crick in the winter," the school trustee warns the young applicant. "Howsumdever, ef you think you kin trust your hide in Flat Crick school-house I ha'n't got no 'bjection." Eggleston's ear for such speech patterns produced one unexpected result. Cultivated Hoosiers of the day were horrified at the book's success in the east and immediately appropriated considerable amounts of money to the state's schools. For a time, in the 1880s, Indiana's per student expenditure for secondary education was among the highest in the nation.

The other serious listener to Hoosier talk in the nineteenth century was James Whitcomb Riley, who wrote in the tradition of dialect poetry from Burns to Dunbar. Riley used a kind of phonetic spelling of his own devising, and some of his poems can be as difficult to read today as Chaucer in the original. Several scholars have questioned the accuracy of Riley's ear, but his work still remains the most ambitious attempt to get everyday speech in Indiana onto the printed page, and it is the one most familiar to readers today.

In this century, Hoosier speech has experienced the same amalgamation and smoothing out of idiosyncracies undergone by regional dialects everywhere, but to the practiced ear, it still retains a distinct quality. Part of this is due to the pronounced nasal tones with which some Hoosiers speak. Kurt Vonnegut, Jr., once said it sounded "like a band saw cutting galvanized tin." The tendency seems to know no boundaries and is as likely to be heard in East Chicago as in Jeffersonville. It may be one of those underlying bonds by which Hoosiers from all parts of the state know each other.

As might be expected, those who were born and raised in Indiana are frequently those who speak in the purest, most distinctive Hoosier manner, using a direct speech almost Biblical in its simplicity and vividness. Precise grammar and exact pronunciation are less important than telling a good story.

A Hoosier who speaks in this characteristic way is Lloyd Stewart, who lives just south of the village of La Fontaine, in Wabash County. La Fontaine was the name of one of the last chiefs of the Miami, the son of a French trader and a Miami princess. From earliest times until the middle of the nineteenth century, this north-central part of the state was prime Indian country. A number of beautiful rivers flow through this area—Mississinewa, Salamonie, Eel, Tippecanoe, and Wildcat—to join eventually with the Wabash. The Miami were the most powerful people along these rivers. There were also Delaware to the south, Wea and Potawatomi to the west, and Huron to the north.

Like the Indians, Lloyd Stewart has hunted just about everything there is to hunt in this part of Indiana—rabbit, squirrel, fox. But his specialty is hunting raccoons. This is how he told about going out hunting one evening with a dog who wouldn't tree:

When I lived up north of Andrews, my youngest son was working up by Gary in the steel mills. And he'd come home over Thanksgiving. I had an old dog, he'd run a coon good. ...But he wouldn't tree. He'd bark-tree it a few times and then leave it, and go back out and run the track some more. He was a good track dog, but he just wasn't no tree dog. Had an awful good purty voice. Bawlin' dog.

One night I had my son let me out....I started following the crick. This old dog went up on the hill and barked a few times. He wouldn't run anything, only a coon. I knew it was a coon he was a-runnin', and it must have been about—oh, I'd say—ten o'clock at night.

He run around all up on the hill. The wind was blowin' pretty strong, and there was a cornfield up on top of the hill, and timber all along the hillside and up on the hill a little ways. But they was a cornfield in west of it, and he got out there in this cornfield. And he boo-hooed and bawled around in there and he couldn't get no place with it. So he came back to where he smelled it there in the woods.

I suppose I fooled around an hour there with him. So I

thought, well, I'll just walk on down, he isn't going to do anything with it. I got him and I took him on down the hill, till it began to run down into level ground. I don't know what that field was in now—I think it was stubble.

But down in the bottom part he got in another little cornfield, and he opened and just raised the dickens in there, barkin', and he went over to the hillside. And he like to ate that tree up, just boo-hooed and bawled, you know, about four or five times, and here he come right back into the cornfield, meetin' me.

Well, I knew he had treed. I took my flashlight out of my pocket and throwed the beam up a tree which was about— oh, probably fourteen to sixteen inches through the butt. It wasn't too high, right on the hillside, the fence right by it. I throwed the light up there and it just looked like a Christmas tree. Never seen so many coon in my life up one tree. I came up and crawled over the fence, and I began to count the coon, and they was eight of them. All grown.

*   *   *

It is the last day of school in Indiana, in late May or early June, and all the flowering trees are in bloom—crab apple and haw, magnolia and tulip poplar, horse chestnut and golden rain tree.

Around the state, in the brick township elementary schools where one's parents once learned their letters and in the elementary wings of the new glass-and-steel consolidated schools which may serve three rural counties, something special is happening. In the feeder schools and junior highs in the shadows of the big-city high schools in Hammond and Evansville and Fort Wayne, in all the fifth and sixth-grade rooms in Delphi and Tell City and Scottsburg, in Decatur and Indianapolis, an old Hoosier ritual is taking place.

The grade-school children have come to pick up their report cards and to say goodbye to their teacher, and on this last morning it is the custom for them to bring along their younger brothers and sisters, the three and four-year-olds, all of them dressed up in their best clothes.

The older children lead them by the hand through the polished hallways and into the strangely quiet home rooms, carefully boosting them up so that they may sit on the desktops and look around and gaze at this wonderful place where their older siblings have spent so much time this past year, and where they, too, in a little while, will be going every day.

It is a serious moment. The teacher, surveying these new faces brimming with expectation and awe, is in a position to see time stretch in both directions: back into the past, into the dim frontier beginnings of Indiana education, the blab schools and one-room schoolhouses, Eggleston's *Hoosier Schoolmaster*, the first normal colleges, the countless Parent Teacher Association meetings and school-board planning sessions, the consolidation struggles of the 1960s, all the dedication and hard work and vision that combined

to make this morning possible; and into the future, since the look in their eyes shows clearly that this is an unbroken chain. Indiana remains a state where older children look forward each year to saying, to their smaller brothers or sisters or next-door neighbors, "It's the last day of school. Take my hand, come with me now, you will see."

*   *   *

It is a perfect summer evening. By seven o'clock we arrive at University Park, two blocks north of Monument Circle in downtown Indianapolis, to watch the fireworks scheduled to go off from the top of the Indiana National Bank tower.

In the meantime, the park fills up with people come to celebrate the nation's birthday and have a good time. Couples stroll about. In a plaza to the north, the electric guitars of a rock band wail. Thin sprays of water rise and fall among dancing bronze figures in the middle of the central fountain. While their mothers watch, children splash and play in the water at the fountain's edge. At least a hundred thousand Hoosiers will gather here this evening—on blankets spread near the fountain and between the flower gardens, sitting on the steps and terraces of the War Memorial to the north, stationed along Meridian and Pennsylvania and other streets that offer a good view.

The display is visible from almost any point in downtown Indianapolis, since the square top of the INB tower, where the rockets are touched off, is thirty-seven stories above street level, or about five hundred feet. (It is the second highest building in Indiana, after the American United Life Building, a few blocks away, which is thirty-eight stories tall, or 533 feet.) Usually, my favorite place to watch the show is from the top of the old clock tower on the Arsenal Building at Arsenal Technical High School, about fifteen blocks east of downtown.

Tech, one of the classic old high schools of Indianapolis—among the others are Crispus Attucks, Shortridge, and Washington—was once a federal arsenal manufacturing munitions during the Civil War. It was converted to a high school in 1911. Annually, a group of teachers climbs to the top of the tower each Fourth of July, taking lawn chairs and picnic supplies with them, in order to have an unsurpassed view of the fireworks issuing from the top of the bank building farther west.

University Park seems the place to be now, along with all the other families and young people. When the original planners laid out the streets of Indianapolis in 1821, among the squares they set aside for markets and public buildings was one intended for a university, should one ever materialize. Several did, but in other parts of the city, and instead University Park is a place of trees and brick walkways and splashing fountains, where office workers sit in the sun eating their lunches, and where statues of Indiana statesmen keep watch through the quiet afternoons.

I have another reason for coming here, too—the shopping bag full of sparklers and small-bore fireworks I bought at a roadside

stand a few days earlier, in anticipation of this evening. During the last few years, these long-prohibited items have suddenly become more available, and all sorts of bottle rockets, fountains, and other exotic whiz-bangs and aerial salutes unknown in my youth are now common items on the folding tables of the streetcorner merchants and sidewalk gypsies who show up everywhere in Indiana at about this time of year.

Who can plumb the mystery of fireworks? Who can explain that fascination? Or the mingling of fear and joy experienced by the six-year-old who, contrary to all his mother's lecturing that morning, reaches out gingerly to receive, from the older boys on the block, a single Black Cat, carefully unwoven from its intricate nest of lethal lookalikes, and now handed over with all the solemnity of a group of scientists dispensing a fresh vial of nitroglycerin?

My mother says that her father knew how to make his own fireworks. He regularly bought the necessary chemicals at a local drugstore and mixed up sufficient quantities of homemade explosives to keep the backyard aglow through half the evenings of those long-ago family celebrations. Back when firecrackers were almost impossible to get, after World War II, I can remember my father on a Fourth of July morning leading me and my cousins out into a vacant lot in order to show us how to make a firecracker out of newspaper and pipe tobacco. He poured out a lid of Prince Albert for all to see and capped the twist of paper with an enormous length of dynamite fuse. Unbeknownst to us, it also had a live dynamite cap crimped on the end which, after we had taken cover, blasted a small crater in the ground.

Now I am a father myself, years later, and there are small children everywhere in the park, their voices ringing with a bright, happy sound which comes from knowing that they will be allowed to stay up late and that something wonderful is going to happen. In company with all these families, my wife and daughter and I find a place in the park, spread our blanket, and bring out the sandwiches and drinks we have brought along. Next we take a stroll along the elevated promenade encircling the War Memorial, and look down on the crowd attending the rock concert.

It is twilight now. In the park below us people begin to light sparklers and toss out strings of ladyfingers. There is a continual fizzing and burning and banging of sound and light everywhere through the trees. Groups of boys crouch around fountains and small rockets, scrambling away when the wicks catch. Columns of silvery white flame rise for a few seconds, leaving vibrant afterimages which are reinforced and overlaid with other brightnesses, other colors. We come back to our spot and rummage through the shopping bag.

First we distribute little flares from China, on sticks, wrapped in tissue paper, with floppy wicks which are hard to get started, which suddenly shoot out intense tongues of flame—yellow, then red, then a most incredible pale blue, followed by white sparks. Out in the street boys are firing fizzy rockets from Coke bottles and the air turns hazy with the smoke of spent powder. All this time daylight leaks away, and the fires we carry and pass among ourselves grow starker, more intense.

I bring out a box of the largest sparklers I have ever seen—the old-fashioned kind, *Made in USA*, on long thick wires with the business portion twelve inches long. They burn for five or six minutes, and I become a conductor, with a baton in each hand, directing the symphony of light all around us. Sparks shower the backs of my hands, needling and prickling. As the big sparklers burn down they reach a point where they warp — make a soft *chink*, like a thin metal rod being tapped on a fence.

Small boys try to wheedle sparklers from us. I pass out a few smaller ones and light their tips. A woman comes by leading a beautiful blonde child of two or three years who is frightened by all the noise and fearful of the sparklers.

"Cain't afford to buy 'em," she explains in a soft, Appalachian accent, "so I bring her down here to see 'em." She grasps the child's hand to keep her from skittering away from the flares we weave back and forth in the air.

It is dark now. There is fire everywhere. This is a festival of light. We are celebrating the solstice—*this arcane knowledge of fire, so lethal, so dangerous, that can see us through long winter nights. The fire of the green tree burning as though alive. The light that one carries, ever fearful.*

Into these mysteries we must be initiated, each of us, one by one, however imperfectly. Put out your hand, take this spark, this coal, and remember. What it has meant to all who have gone before. To all those yet to come. Let us play with it now, in the darkness, let us dance and show each other this miracle.

I take a small sparkler, light it, and hand it to the woman, who places it in the child's hands and closes her fingers about the wire. Sparks pelt her skin. She thrusts it away as though it will consume her. The mother coaxes and soothes. The child's eyes are filled with light. I hear the mother's voice speaking in wonder.

Someone else asks for a sparkler, and at that moment I carelessly touch the middle part of the wire I am holding, which has just gone out. Pain sears my fingers. When I look up, the woman and child are gone. There is a great lingering boom high above us, announcing the beginning of the fireworks on the bank tower.

In the park and along the streets everyone accepts the fizz of the first skyrocket as a challenge. We light and throw and hold up everything we have left, and for a moment, engulfed by brilliant flashes and bursts of color, we see each other and everything around us with great clarity. ∎

Right: Soybeans in the east-central portion of the state near Muncie. Imported from China in the 1920s, the soybean became, after corn, the state's second most important cash crop.

Above: Three important figures in Tippecanoe County history share a pediment on the courthouse at Lafayette — General William Henry Harrison, the Marquis de Lafayette, and Shawnee statesman Tecumseh. *Left:* Dancer at the "Festival of the Turning Leaves" in Thorntown, Boone County, once the site of a Miami Indian reservation. *Overleaf:* The First Mennonite Chuch, 1912, in Berne, east-central Indiana.

The Culver Black Horse Troop leads student units of artillery and infantry in the last dress parade of the year at Culver Military Academy, a coeducational college preparatory school on the shores of Lake Maxinkuckee, Marshall County. Formed in 1897, the cavalry unit is a familiar sight in parades around the country and has appeared in celebrations accompanying eight presidential inaugurations.

Above: At the heart of the University of Notre Dame campus near South Bend stands the statue of Father Edward Sorin, who came from Vincennes with seven Holy Cross brothers to found the college in 1842. In the background rises the Administration Building's golden dome, the University's most recognizable landmark. *Overleaf:* Wetlands in northern Indiana, southeast of Lake Wawasee in Kosciusko County.

North of Fort Wayne, in the Auburn-Cord-Duesenberg Museum at Auburn, master-pieces preserved from Indiana's automobile-manufacturing past are exhibited in a style befitting their original splendor. Now on the National Register of Historic Places, the Auburn factory's art deco showrooms house the collection and serve as the center of the classic car festival held each Labor Day weekend.

Above: A musket fusillade salutes the raising of the flag in front of Fort Wayne's reconstructed military post. History buffs costumed as American, British, and French soldiers reenact episodes from the city's frontier period. *Overleaf:* Spending weekends at the family cottage is a northern Indiana tradition. This is High Lake, between Columbia City and Kendallville in Noble County. The Merry Lea Nature Preserve borders the lake on the north and west.

Hot-air balloons tug at their lines at the beginning of a race during the Three Rivers Festival. Held each July in Fort Wayne, the week-long schedule of parades, dancing, concerts, and theater performances celebrates the city's rich cultural and ethnic traditions. Included in the fun is a popular competition watched by thousands — a build-it-yourself raft race down the Saint Joseph River.

The state tree, the tulip poplar, also called the yellow poplar, belongs to the magnolia family and produces showy, yellow blossoms which shrink to dense seedpods by autumn. Trees are everywhere in Indiana, from the lush golden rain trees of New Harmony to the monumental ginkgoes of Lockerbie Square. Over one hundred and thirty species may be studied in their natural settings in nineteen state parks.

Alternate sources of energy—currently receiving considerable attention as Indiana's manufacturers and corporations concentrate on sophisticated new technologies—have never really gone out of fashion in rural areas. On this Fulton County farm near Rochester, a repairman goes up to check the balky rotor of a windmill installed to pump water for a farmer's beef cattle.

Drive off the Interstate, leave the blacktop road, head out into the backcountry almost anywhere in Indiana on a bright afternoon in July or August, and this is what you will find: a fertile green world where cultivated crops and natural plants come together in carefully blanced profusion. In the foreground, white Queen Anne's lace and small blue cornflowers bloom together.

Near Rochester in Fulton County, lies Lake Manitou, named in honor of the great spirit of the Chippewa Indians. At several large reservoirs constructed throughout the state in the 1960s, and at hundreds of freshwater lakes left behind by the glaciers in the northeast, Hoosiers have ample opportunity each summer to relax and enjoy themselves by swimming, sailing, waterskiing, and fishing.

Above: Battleground near Lafayette. Here, in 1811, William Henry Harrison's army stopped an alliance of resurgent Indian tribes headed by Tecumseh and the Prophet. The victory inspired the "Tippecanoe and Tyler too!" rallying cry which helped Harrison reach the White House thirty years later. *Overleaf:* A no-frills barn exemplifies the style of Amish life in northern Indiana.

Above: A traditional small-town refuge from summer's heat and glare, this perfectly preserved movie theater, built in 1939, still attracts young patrons in Garrett, north of Fort Wayne. *Right:* A bedroom in author Gene Stratton Porter's Geneva home, now a state memorial. *Overleaf:* Catwalk in Michigan City Harbor leading out to the New Lighthouse, Indiana's only operating lighthouse.

Above: On their transcontinental migrations, sandhill cranes make a major rest stop in the wetlands of the Jasper-Pulaski State Fish and Wildlife Area. *Left:* Weekend *voyageurs* of the Ouiatenon Brigade beach their canoe on the banks of the Wabash River near Huntington. *Overleaf:* The Great Mound in Mounds State Park, Anderson. At least two thousand years old, it is the largest single prehistoric earthwork in Indiana.

An autumn afternoon in Rocky Hollow, a box canyon cut deeply into the sandstone narrows of Turkey Run State Park near Rockville. One of the state's most scenic parks, it is the second oldest and was acquired in 1916 with public and private funds raised by Richard Lieber, father of the Indiana park system. In the drive to buy the land, a major donation came from the Indianapolis Motor Speedway.

Brackets cut with a scroll saw provide the only decoration on the front porch of this hundred-year-old farmhouse south of Michigan City in LaPorte County. Balloon-frame construction, using walls made with two-by-fours, became the dominant method of homebuilding in Indiana after the Civil War. This house, constructed by the grandfather of the present owner, has been handed down through the generations.

Looking as sturdy as the day it was opened in 1882, the Narrows Covered Bridge spans Sugar Creek in the western part of the state. Partially hidden by the wooden structure is the concrete arch of a new bridge leading into Turkey Run State Park. During the ten-day Parke County Covered Bridge Festival in October, visitors take four different tours of the county's thirty-five historic bridges.

Sycamores in a backyard in the town of Winchester, east of Muncie and a few miles from the Ohio line. If the tulip is the official tree, the sycamore remains a popular favorite. The chorus of the state song written by Paul Dresser, brother of novelist Theodore Dreiser, reminds homesick Hoosiers that it is "... through the sycamores, the candlelights are gleaming / On the banks of the Wabash, far away."

Atop blocks of limestone in the momentarily quiescent Sutphin Fountain at the main entrance to the Indianapolis Museum of Art, thin sheets of water not yet warmed by the sun mirror the blue of the morning sky. The Museum's collections and pavilions reflect a century of Hoosier generosity in the form of gifts from families such as Lilly, Krannert, Clowes, Noyes, Pantzer, Holliday, and Eiteljorg.

Above: "Hoosier Hysteria" reaches a peak during the championship game of the boys' state basketball tournament at Market Square Arena in downtown Indianapolis. The tournament is classless, pitting large schools against small, country against city, and upstate against downstate for four weekends of elimination play in March. *Overleaf:* Looking east on Washington Street: a view of the Indianapolis skyline.

Above: Seconds after hearing the command, "Gentlemen, start your engines!" Indy's best drivers move out in eleven rows of three cars each and hold this formation until they receive the green flag to start the race. *Right:* World-class natatorium on the campus of Indiana University-Purdue University at Indianapolis. *Overleaf:* The school's Olympic-caliber track and field stadium.

Above: Reconstruction of the farmhouse near Millville where aviation pioneer Wilbur Wright was born in 1867. *Left:* Grand prix jumping, one of the most difficult events of the annual Traders Point Hunt Charity Horse Show in Zionsville. *Overleaf:* Oldenburg, a hilltop village of red brick buildings and slender spires, was built by German Catholic immigrants in the nineteenth century.

Above: Harness racing at the Shelby County Fair. A car from one of the midway rides floats like an escaped pinwheel above the wooden grandstand. *Right:* Lightning rods and weathervane on the cupola of a barn in northern Marion County, between the villages of Augusta and New Augusta. Artifact of a vanished world, today the barn is surrounded on all sides by subdivisions.

Above: Trees near Brookville, county seat of Franklin County, in the Whitewater River Valley of eastern Indiana. Brookville provided so many of Indiana's early leaders it was called "the cradle of statesmen." *Left:* The kitchen of Ernie Pyle's boyhood home, now a state memorial in Dana. Pyle, beloved correspondent of World War II, received a Pulitzer Prize in 1944 and was killed by sniper fire in 1945.

Above: At the Portland Arch Nature Preserve in Fountain County, Bear Creek has carved a sandstone tunnel eight feet high. *Right:* In 1967 the Indiana State Museum took up residence in the former Indianapolis City Hall, which was built in 1909. At the rear on the second floor is the seal of the State of Indiana. *Overleaf:* Meharry Hall, built in 1877, in DePauw University's East College, Greencastle.

VISIT THE
PHILADELPHIA
CENTENNIAL

1876 · MAY · 1876

S M T W T F S
           1 2 3 4 5 6
7 8 9 10 11 12 13
14 15 16 17 18 19 20
21 22 23 24 25 26 27
28 29 30 31

Above: "And the maple-bright Indiana / noon was the color of bonfires," remembers contemporary poet Philip Appleman. *Left:* Reconstructed laboratory where, in 1876, Colonel Eli Lilly started what became one of the world's largest pharmaceutical companies. *Overleaf:* Farm near Eagle Creek Park, whose forty-five hundred acres in northwest Indianapolis make it one of the nation's biggest municipal parks.

A balloon race at sunrise signals the opening of the Indiana State Fair. Described as "one of the real farmland state fairs with everything from rooster-crowing to husband-calling contests," it draws enormous crowds for ten days in late August and offers Hoosiers from around the state a chance to celebrate the past year's accomplishments in farming, homemaking, crafts, and manufacturing.

Above: Indianapolis families waiting for the beginning of the Fourth of July fireworks arrange rows of lawnchairs across the mall between buildings housing the National Headquarters of the American Legion. The pyramid-topped structure at the center of their view is the Indiana World War Memorial, dedicated to veterans of World War I. *Overleaf:* Springtime on the Circle.

Masters of Fox Hounds, staff, and foxhounds, followed by ladies and gentlemen with colors, parade on their way to the annual blessing of the hounds at the Traders Point Hunt clubhouse. Next comes the casting of the hounds and the season's first hunt. Elsewhere in the state, abundant quantities of quail, pheasant, and deer make hunting an extremely popular pastime for many Hoosiers.

A lamb born the previous spring and four adult sheep ready for shearing. While much of Indiana's wool crop goes to commercial outlets, local spinners and weavers provide a steady market for quality fiber. Displays of weaving and other traditional crafts may be seen annually at the Indiana State Fair and at the Penrod Festival, the Talbott Street Art Fair, and the Broad Ripple Art Fair.

The official state bird. Members of the finch family, cardinals mate for life and are extremely territorial. They became state birds in 1933 after the Indiana Historical Bureau commended their "rich and cheery song...heard in Indiana all year long." Also official in Indiana are the peony (state flower), "Indiana" by Arthur Mapes of Kendallville (state poem), and limestone (state stone).

The home of lumber baron John August Reitz, completed 1872, maintains its opulence in Evansville's Historic Preservation District which is located along the Ohio River. Formerly the lumber capital of the world, Evansville is now the major industrial, transportation and trade center of Southern Indiana.

"Great things have been effected by a few men well conducted—our cause is just—our country will be grateful." The George Rogers Clark National Memorial at Vincennes. The surprise victory here of Clark's army of Long Knives over the British in 1779 assured American control of the northwest territories. Erected on the site of the old fort, the memorial was dedicated by Franklin Delano Roosevelt in 1936.

Above: The Culbertson Mansion, jewel of mansion row in New Albany, across the Ohio River from Louisville. During the Civil War period, shipyards in New Albany and nearby Jeffersonville were important producers of paddlewheel steamboats. The *Rob't E. Lee,* famous for its race against the *Natchez,* was built here in 1866. *Overleaf:* Tobacco, a major cash crop in southern Indiana.

Contestants train for months gearing up for the Little 500 Bicycle Race in April at Indiana University in Bloomington. It is an endurance relay, with four-man teams pedaling one bike for fifty miles. Steve Tesich, originally from East Chicago, drew on his undergraduate racing experiences here to create the highly successful film *Breaking Away*, which received an Academy Award for best screenplay.

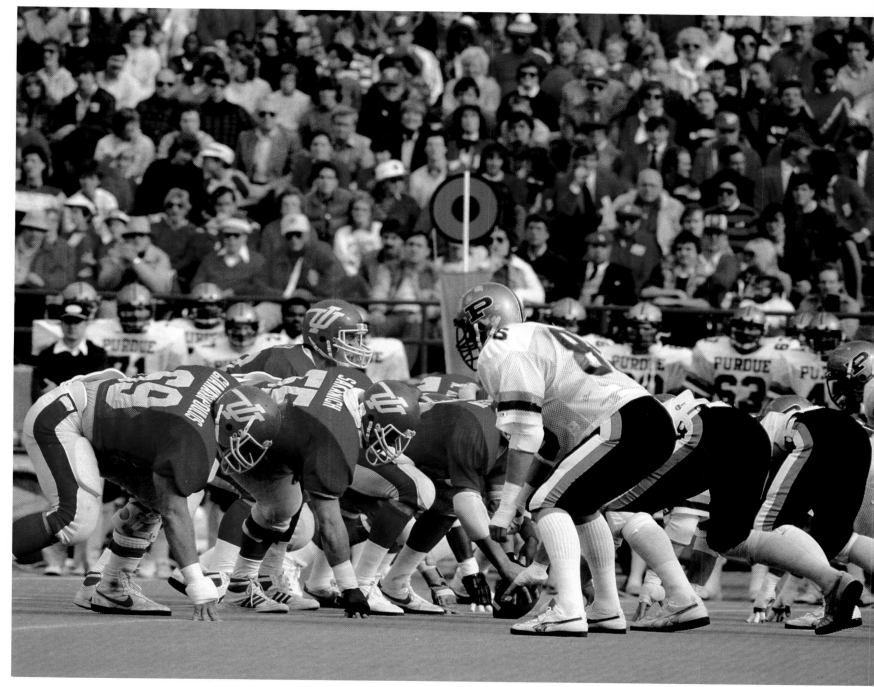

Above: The IU Hoosiers square off against the Purdue Boilermakers in the state's fiercest gridiron rivalry—the victor will add a link to the Old Oaken Bucket trophy. Elsewhere, Wabash battles DePauw for the Monon Bell, and the Butler Bulldogs and Indiana Central Greyhounds slug it out to see who is top dog. *Overleaf:* Big Clifty Falls, one of five different waterfalls at Clifty Falls State Park near Madison.

Brown County becomes a showcase of natural brilliance in the fall, and driving there to view the leaves is an annual tradition for many Hoosiers. The best overlooks are to be found in Brown County State Park, near the county seat of Nashville. With its 15,543 acres, the park is by far the state's largest and offers extensive hiking trails and facilities for camping, swimming, and riding.

Above: Visitors to the state memorial at Metamora travel by horse-drawn canal boat along a restored section of Whitewater Canal. By 1848, the Canal reached seventy-six miles from Lawrenceburg to Hagerstown, but railroads soon outmoded it. *Overleaf:* The Lanier Mansion in Madison, designed by Francis Costigan in 1844. A banker, Lanier arranged loans to help Indiana avert bankruptcy during the Civil War.

Hillforest Mansion, high above the Ohio River and the town of Aurora, in Dearborn County. Built in 1852, in the style of an Italian Renaissance villa, its proximity to the River and the resemblance of its rounded porch and cupola to a pilot house, identify it as "steamboat gothic" to many of the visitors who come here. The cupola offers a commanding view of the river valley below.

Confederate artillerymen charge their piece during a reenactment of "The Siege of Vernon," honoring the only town in Indiana that Morgan's Raiders could not take. Encountering fierce resistance from the home guards, and realizing that federal troops were only a few hours behind him, Morgan deployed his force south and east of Vernon and went on to plunder five more towns before crossing into Ohio.

"When the frost is on the punkin and the fodder's in the shock." So James Whitcomb Riley began one of his most popular poems. Cornstalks in Riley's day were gathered into standing bundles, or shocks, and taken from the field as needed, to be chopped up and fed to livestock. Today, on farms like this one in eastern Indiana, the stalks are shredded during harvesting and returned to the land.

Fishermen with a reserve tank to fill, houseboaters come for the morning paper, canoeists looking for a cup of coffee—everyone near Aurora and out on the Ohio River today will stop here or at least wave as they go by. Locks and dams set up to control flooding along the Ohio have expanded the shoreline, creating new waterfront acreage and stimulating homebuilding and recreation.

Above: A water-powered gristmill operates daily in the Pioneer Village at Spring Mill State Park near Bedford. In the right foreground, is the mill's two-story log house. *Right:* The falls at McCormick's Creek State Park, east of Spencer. *Overleaf:* Emblems of a rough-hewn world, even the shutter hinges on the window of this reconstructed cabin in the Lincoln Boyhood National Memorial near Gentryville are made of wood.

Above: Harrison County's courthouse, built in Corydon in 1811, was the state capitol from 1813 to 1825. The first Indiana Constitution was written in this room in June of 1816. *Left:* One of the largest domed Romanesque churches in the country may be seen at the Convent of the Immaculate Conception at Ferdinand. *Overleaf:* David Dale Owen's Gothic Revival house and laboratory at New Harmony date from 1859.

Above: Columbus, midwestern mecca of contemporary architecture, attracts thousands of people yearly who view the city's buildings such as this Indiana Bell switching center designed by Paul Kennon in 1978. *Right:* Union troops present arms at Vernon. *Overleaf:* Greensburg after dark. Across the street, but not visible here is the town's trademark, a tree growing from the courthouse tower.

Above: The Knobs, a range of extremely eroded, cone-shaped hills fanned out between Scottsburg and Salem in the southern part of Indiana. Hoosier hikers and backpackers following the fifty-seven-mile Knobstone Trail encounter this view of the Knobs at the north end of the trail in Jackson-Washington State Forest near Brownstown. *Left:* Indian summer, the best time of the year in the Hoosier State.

FURTHER READING

A good overall view is offered by *Indiana: A Guide to the Hoosier State,* compiled by workers of the Writers' Program of the Work Projects Administration in the State of Indiana and published by Oxford University Press in 1941; there have been several reprintings. It is supplemented by *The Calumet Region Historical Guide,* also compiled by the Indiana WPA and published in Gary by Garman Printing in 1939. A thoroughly updated sequel to these two books is scheduled for distribution by the Indiana Historical Society in 1985.

Among single-volume histories, William E. Wilson's *Indiana: A History* (Bloomington: Indiana University Press, 1966) heads the list, followed closely by Howard H. Peckham's *Indiana: A History* (New York: Norton, 1978). *Indianapolis: The Story of a City* (Indianapolis: Bobbs-Merrill, 1971), by Edward A. Leary, concentrates on the state's capital, while James B. Lane's *"City of the Century"* (Indiana University Press, 1978) deals with Gary. *Indiana* (New York: Coward-McCann, 1969), by Jeannette C. Nolan, is a useful book for secondary-school students.

Bibliographies in the adult histories should be consulted for references to more extensive surveys and for books on the state's agriculture and industry; for more specialized studies, such as works on the prehistoric mounds, native peoples, and New Harmony; and for biographies of the major political figures, such as George Rogers Clark, Tecumseh, and Eugene Debs. See also the back files of *Indiana Magazine of History, Outdoor Indiana,* and *The Hoosier State: Readings in Indiana History,* a two-volume set edited by Ralph Gray, issued by Eerdmans Publishing in Grand Rapids in 1980 and subsequently by Indiana University Press.

A number of oversized illustrated histories provide helpful introductions to Indiana history and culture. Chief among these is *A Pictorial History of Indiana* (Indiana University Press, 1980) by Dwight W. Hoover, with Jane Rodman. Edward A. Leary's *Indianapolis: A Pictorial History* (Virginia Beach: Donning, 1980) and George Geib's *Indianapolis: Hoosiers' Circle City* (Tulsa, Oklahoma: Continental Heritage Press, 1981) are more specialized. A similar volume is *The Fort Wayne Story: A Pictorial History* (Woodland Hills, California: Windsor, 1980) by John Ankenbruck.

Indiana's literary heritage is surveyed by Arthur Shumaker's *A History of Indiana Literature* (Indianapolis: Indiana Historical Society, 1962). Comprehensive biographic and bibliographic information from the territorial period to 1980 is supplied by the three volumes of *Indiana Authors and their Books* (Crawfordsville: Wabash College, 1949, 1974, 1980). The first volume was compiled by R. E. Banta, the last two by Donald E. Thompson. Two important samplers, both from Indiana University Press, are *Hoosier Caravan: A Treasury of Indiana Life and Lore* (second edition, 1975), selected by R. E. Banta, and *The Indiana Experience* (1977), edited by A. L. Lazarus.

An indispensable study of Indiana art is Wilbur D. Peat's *Pioneer Painters of Indiana* (Indianapolis: Art Association of Indianapolis, 1974). Peat's *Indiana Houses of the Nineteenth Century* (Indiana Historical Society, 1962) is complemented by *Indianapolis Architecture* (Indianapolis: Indiana Architecture Foundation, 1975), the work of a number of hands. Valuable studies of Indiana crafts are Pauline Montgomery's *Indiana Coverlet Weavers and their Coverlets* (Indianapolis: Hoosier Heritage Press, 1974) and Kathleen R. Postle's *The Chronicle of the Overbeck Pottery* (Indiana Historical Society, 1978).

Hoosier Folk Legends (1982), compiled by Ronald L. Baker, and *Indiana Folklore: A Reader* (1980), edited by Linda Degh, are both from Indiana University Press. Leah Jackson Wolford's *The Play-Party in Indiana* (Indiana Historical Society, 1917 and 1959) and Paul G. Brewster's *Ballads and Songs of Indiana* (Indiana University Press, 1940; New York: Folklorica, 1981) are important early studies of Indiana folk culture. A more recent examination of folklore in the Calumet Region is Richard M. Dorson's *Land of the Millrats* (Cambridge: Harvard, 1981).

Two related books dealing with everyday Hoosier speech are *Indiana Place Names* (Indiana University Press, 1975) by R. L. Baker and Marvin Carmony and *Indiana Dialects in their Historical Setting* (Terre Haute: Indiana Council Teachers of English, 1972) by Marvin Carmony.

The photographs of Frank Hohenberger are featured in *If You Don't Outdie Me: The Legacy of Brown County* (Indiana University Press, 1982), by Dillon Bustin. Also see *Southern Indiana* (Indiana University Press, 1965), with photographs by Hartley Alley and text by Jean Alley.

A booklet, *Indiana Ragtime,* by John Hasse and Frank Gillis, which accompanies a two-record documentary album of the same name issued by the Indiana Historical Society in 1981, is useful on the subject of early popular music. Duncan Schiedt's *The Jazz State of Indiana* (Pittsboro, Indiana: Duncan Schiedt, 1977) covers the period from World War I to the 1950s. A relevant biography is Hoagy Carmichael's *Stardust Road* (New York: Rinehart, 1946).

Bob Williams' *Hoosier Hysteria!* (South Bend: Icarus Press, 1982) continues the coverage of Indiana highschool basketball begun by Herb Schwomeyer, whose history of the same subject, also called *Hoosier Hysteria,* from Mitchell-Fleming Publishers in Greenfield, went through five editions by 1982. Contrasting views of another important sporting event are provided by Al Boemker's *500 Miles to Go: The Story of the Indianapolis Speedway* (New York: Coward-McCann, 1961) and Ron Dorson's *The Indy 500: An American Institution Under Fire* (Newport Beach, California: Bond/Parkhurst, 1974).

Contemporary reflections on Indiana's people and history are provided by Irving Leibowitz in *My Indiana* (Englewood Cliffs, New Jersey: 1964), Tom Keating in *Indiana Faces and Other Places* (Indianapolis: Indiana Only Press, 1982), and Bob Collins in *Thought You'd Never Ask* (South Bend: Icarus Press, 1984).

Exploring Indianapolis (Indianapolis: Lexicon, 1982) by Nancy Kriplen and Margaret Winter is a comprehensive sight-seer's guide to the city. *Indiana: A Guide to State Forests, State Parks, Reservoirs, State Fish and Wildlife Areas,* published by the Department of Natural Resources in 1983, lists sites and available facilities for camping and related activities. *Indiana Always,* published annually by a firm of the same name in Greenwood, offers concise statewide tourist information. *The Indiana Wanderbook,* also an annual, is distributed free of charge by the Tourism Development Division of the Indiana Department of Commerce.